She - The Sultana

AF368845

Dr. Zainab Ansari

BOOK-O-PEDIA PUBLICATION

(AFFILIATED TO SUBHARAMBH PUBLICATION HOUSE)
KRIYA YOGA ASHRAM LANE, LOKANATH VIHAR
DAMODAR ROAD, PURI, 752001, ODISHA
Email: bookopediapublication@gmail.com
Instagram:
https://www.instagram.com/bookopedia_publication/

COPYRIGHT © Dr. Zainab Ansari, 2022
All rights reserved. No part of this book may be reproduced, stored in a retrieval system, or transmitted, in any form by any means, Electronic, Mechanical, Magnetic, Optical, Chemical, Manual, Photocopying, Recording or otherwise (Except for mention in reviews or edited excerpts in the media) without the prior written consent of its writer and publisher.

This is a work of fiction. Names, characters, places and incidents are either product of the author's imagination or are used fictitiously and any resemblance to any actual person, living or dead, events or locales is purely coincidental.

"SHE-THE SULTANA"
ISBN: 978-93-5504-095-4
FICTION 1st Edition
TYPESETTING BY: SUSMITA SWAIN
COVER DESIGN: SUBHAM DEV KUMAR

The opinions/ contents expressed in this book are solely of the author and do not represent the opinions/ standings/ thought of publisher

INTRODUCTION

I never understood the power of words until they transformed my soul from withering to blooming.

PREFACE

This book is an affirmation book, that
healing does happen, if you have the will
power to move beyond your numbness and
change into your power.
Especially dedicated to the women who are
unable to raise a voice.
I am here for you.

ACKNOWLEDGEMENT

This book would have not been possible
without the encouragement of my parents,
the lessons and life experiences and all the
souls who genuinely love and cherish me.

DISCLAIMER

The book is a work of poetry.
This book is a collective work of the
contributing author and the publisher. The
author is the sole copyright owner of the
work she/he has contributed to this project
and retains all right to her work.

ABOUT THE AUTHOR

Dr. Zainab Ansari is a professor, writer,
poetess, podcaster, author and co-author of
several anthologies.
Her words can be read on Instagram on
@whitepurplezainu.
Words have been savior no matter which life
phase she stood at.

She has crumbled in the ball of madness and sanity when the pain of soul wrenching memories took over but she released a breath of calmness, inhaling sanity and exhaling freakiness.

My dear readers……

My word connection souls…...

The empty pages provided are for

Penning down your thought and
feelings…...

After you read the poem….

Let these poems be your balm to grow
and heal.

PORES OF EXCELLENCE

Her origins and aura,
are very simple and humble,
the fear in her,
has broken the chains of self-sacrifice,
she has learnt to leap and fly,
with the wings of courage,
that have a scent of gratitude lingering in the
glory pores,
of her excellence.

HEALER

Her existence is blessed,
she is a healer,
who inhales the bad demonic stench of
darkness,
to transform the venom into pure life elixir,
she tastes the pain and blows the wounded
soul,
with the potion of her kind nurturing blood,
she drinks the acid that runs in the veins of
dying,
to only fill them with her love,
without sabotaging her precious,
endangered soul and life.

CARNIVAL

Her eyes hold,
the vibrant sparks,
of a memorable carnival,
that is a dawn.
to the depths of dusk,
that blooms like blushing blossoms,
with the ignition of shy lava.

BLOOD

Her ink is the blood,
that bonded and decorated the words,
with reels of emotions, pride and magnolia
feelings,
her breaths are stories and verses of
magnificence,
that held universes as grand as solar system,
as minute as a grain of mustard.

EPITOME

She is the epitome,
of the black ugly scars that have healed in
her garden of life,
that bled red and pink pain,
from among the clouds of cracks and holes,
of the destination and journeys that the rain
of burden swept,
while glowing from the sparkling light of
direction and growth.

REVOLUTION

She wore her smile and crown,
like the revolution,
that were shaped,
like her pure tears,
she was the flux and flex of life,
as she pledged her soul,
that life and trials had reformed her,
that no matter how her heart had been
stabbed,
beyond words and infinity,
she had bloomed to be a woman of rhyme
and rhythm,
who was far more than,
the poet that breathed emotions and
exquisiteness,
she was the warmth of existence whose
mantra,
had changed from self-sacrifice to self-
respect.

TURQUOISE AND TEAL

She is a mix,
of turquoise and teal,
fragmented anger shards,
that colored her smile to lavender amethyst
waves,
she was filled with colors of wilderness,
that had and still the scent of blood,
in her autumns and winter modes of power,
she is a free emblem,
that disconnects from the bards and chains
of demonic negativity,
she ignites like the courageous and bold
paper, pen and sword,
she is after all the colorful weaver of pearls,
that scream out decency and beauty.

PEARL

TEACHER

She is not only a remarkable woman,
but a teacher and mentor in her own manner,
her existence is a lesson in itself,
to the ones around her who she really is,
a woman of greatness,
she lets the buds near her,
bloom and expand,
from the nectar of her love and light,
she inspires the watchers to grow despite the
tag line of being impossible in many
situations,
she is an unsung hero and queen,
among the various celebrated and
unrecognized power houses,
she shapes the lives and directs the journey
of rainbow, rain and sunshine,
with the power and strength of standing firm
and respecting the aura within.

BOUNTY

She is a treasure,
a woman of precious rareness,
a bounty with virtues of wisdom,
and humbleness as the blood of her veins,
she is the root of life that acknowledges the
seeds of compassion,
with the knowledge of growth and
versatility,
within the numbness of coldness of the
world,
by regaining and maintain her spark of being
aflame for herself and the ones absorbing
her earth.

MUSE

She smiles,
and extends her hands,
to the circle of empowering women around
her,
her circle is small,
but filled with quality and power,
the strength of sisterhood and hard work,
being their honor and pride,
they breathe in each other's liquid energy,
that is invisible to the world but the rays and
waves are felt by their pores,
they linked into the bond and loop of
resonating aura,
the cloak of loyalty and compassion,
they are the nurturing earth with the passion
of fire of life,
they are the cleansing water with the ever
vibrant air,
they are women who celebrate each soul on
this earth,
especially the women who are silent
between pages on danger.

DANDELION

She is a wild dandelion,
that has learnt its value,
she grows and glows alone,
and blows until she decorates the lands of
far and near,
she is a traveler with the desire to breathe in,
the multitudes of environmental treasures,
of this very mother earth whose womb
resembles her love for nurturing,
she escalates the mountains of literal beauty
and metaphorical burdens,
she descends the seas of depth into the
bloodlines that are never still,
she is ever alive and vibrant,
always on the flow of life.

LEGEND

She is a legend,
she is glory,
much more than the ever-visible skin and
bones,
she is more sweeter than the November and
far colder in December,
she is a mixture of seasons and months,
she holds passion, tricks, tips and treats,
that can never be boxed into compartment,
as she evolves,
from uniqueness into an axis of her own tilt
and rotation.

She is a perfume, a scent that fragrances the
environment she blooms in.

www.ingramcontent.com/pod-product-compliance
Lightning Source LLC
LaVergne TN
LVHW092036190726
843493LV00002B/714